TWILIGHT SCRIBBLES

STRAY THOUGHTS ON THE WORLD AROUND US

GIRIJA THEKKINKATIL

Copyright © Girija Thekkinkatil
All Rights Reserved.

This book has been published with all efforts taken to make the material error-free after the consent of the author. However, the author and the publisher do not assume and hereby disclaim any liability to any party for any loss, damage, or disruption caused by errors or omissions, whether such errors or omissions result from negligence, accident, or any other cause.

While every effort has been made to avoid any mistake or omission, this publication is being sold on the condition and understanding that neither the author nor the publishers or printers would be liable in any manner to any person by reason of any mistake or omission in this publication or for any action taken or omitted to be taken or advice rendered or accepted on the basis of this work. For any defect in printing or binding the publishers will be liable only to replace the defective copy by another copy of this work then available.

Dedicated to my daughters Anjana and Varada

Contents

Contents

Contents

Foreword

It is said a poet has the unique gift of gazing at life through images and metaphors, and this is true of Girija Thekkinkatil. Her poems show a wide range of themes varying from nature, love, real-life -situations, environment, metaphysics to science and the cyber world. An agriculture scientist by profession, she introduces a sort of scientific discipline into her poems. Some poems celebrate nature and some others are subjective outpourings. A few other poems are thought-provoking and illuminate the mind of readers. She often laments the damage caused to nature by man and exhorts her readers to save the planet. Her poems are short, some even if shorter but all express profound thoughts in simple style and are fully rooted in reality. Her apt use of epithets, pithy observation, refreshing creativity and subtle humour make her poems highly readable.

Professor Brinda Moorthy

Retd. Principal, Govt. Victoria College,

Palakkad, Kerala, India

Preface

As a teenager writing poems was an outlet for the little stressses I experienced. As a busy mother and a teacher never had the time to analyse my thoughts. Now during the twilight of my life, relieved of both personal and official duties, I have been scribbling my observations, outlook and aspirations.With the encouragement of my readers' I share them for your perusal. I hope it will give you as much pleasure as I experienced while scribbling the same.

Acknowledgements

My life's journey would never have been so smooth but for the love and support from my husband, E. Vijayaraghavan. Thank you for being there for me and encouraging my rattles with your critical comments. Without your encouragement and support, this humble venture would never have seen the light of the day. I also acknowledge my grandchildren Rithika and Dhruv for all the inspiration, family and friends for their love and support. I bow before the Lord Almighty for making this dream come true.

1. Wonders of Nature

Sleep my baby sleep
Sleep my baby sleep
To go around the world in your dream
Off we go to see the wonders of nature
To see the sunrise at Tiger hill
And the sunset at Kanyakumari
Go to the beaches for a holiday
Climb the mountains for a break
Visit the zoo to see the animals
And the aquarium for the fishes
Forget your tablets and your phones
Look around to feel the joy of life
Alas! You can do all this only in your sleep
*Till '**Corona**' leaves the world*
So sleep my baby sleep
To go around the world in your dreams

This poem was penned during the lockdown

2. Bonsai

I am a banyan tree
In a bonsai dish
People feel it's a game
I feel it's a shame
To grow me in a pot
Treat me like a little tot
Birds don't linger by my side
Branches offer no roosting site
Can't put me in a village square
Nor in a temple complex
People don't gossip around
Squirrels don't jump about
No shade for passers by
No shelter from heat or cold
I am just a miniature
And not the whole

3. Lock Down Lessons

Country in lockdown
People in quarantine
Face mask a compulsion
Hugs and kisses out of fashion
Handshake no longer a salutation
Namaste a better option
Family and friends a distant vision
Dialing them is the only recreation
Teaching a virtual mission
Learning a leisurely action
Tours and travels no longer a temptation
Pubs and parties all forgotten
Dating and chatting an online mission
Junk food holds no attention
Home food a major attraction
Work from home a tedious session
Money in the bank only compensation

4. MySelf

I am a scientist
Who speaks of plants
Daughter tells me
She is not a fan
Plants and parasites not her cup or can
I switch to poetry
For my kids and clan
To express myself as much as I can.

5. Retirement

It's time to say goodbye
To friends and foes alike
To forget and forgive one and all
Relive and relent bygone days
Tiresome days, sleepless nights
Treacherous peers, endless calls
Terrifying reviews, tedious travels
Midnight oil spent on files
Endless meetings, restless life
Adieu to one and all
All these for you to hold
Happily I leave you all
To chase a passion kept on hold

6. Ode to the Moving Clouds

As I sit on my porch
I see clouds passing by
Will they halt for me to talk
'Nay' they say
"We are in mission mode
Have to rush
And reach the mountains with all our might
A little wind may sometimes help
Most of the time we push ourselves"
I feel so sad I have nowhere to go
I try to tell the marching clouds
The route they follow is not the normal course
The rain they carry is not to soak
Give our share before you go
Sprinkle a little on the roads
Bring a smile to thirsty folks
They hardly wait to hear me out
Ahead they troop with little care
Ready to cause havoc
In places I don't know where

7. Climate Change

Season is on, seeds are sown

See no rains for crop to grow

Rains are scarce, drought is more

Summers hot, winters freezing cold

'Climate change' the word for these woes

Cut the trees, clear the woods

Clog the drains, dirty the oceans

Burn the trash and spoil the air

It's payback time and nothing more

Garner courage to hoot into 'Ozone hole'

Scan the pacific for 'Garbage float'

Mend your ways or see your children grow

In plastic land where nothing grows

8. Exam Fear

Sitting in the exam hall
My hands tremble
Numbness spreads from toes
Everything seems to fall apart
Am I going to pass out
Master comes with a smiling face
Serves the paper for me to write
Sees the panic on my face
Thumbs my shoulder to boost me up
Scan the paper before I start
Not so bad as I thought
Pen is the master, travels fast
Answers seem to flow out
At times it tumbles past
Questions difficult to crack apart
Alas! Time is up
And I finish my exam at last.

9. Time Machine Please

If I had a time machine
To go back and forth in life
To relive the moments we cherished
To be with friends we missed
To remedy the mistakes we made
To tell the words we never said
Colorful dreams do sometimes come
Take me out for treat and fun
Give a chance to meet loved ones
They end so fast I feel bereft
To leave the group so abrupt
Yet I feel refreshed
To be with friends I least expect

10. What For

I wonder why I feel so sad
As I sit gazing upon you lad
The sunken eyes, matted hair
Weathered shirt and broken bowl
Asks for food or speaks against the war
The fight for might, fight for right
Fight to gain what's not theirs
Treacherous tanks, deadly missiles
Bombing planes and nightly black outs
Yet we claim to be civilized
Let us work for a peaceful life
Save the people from this senseless plight
Fill the world with love and light

11. Daily Dose

Senior citizen is a jerk
With a single toast for breakfast
To keep the system vigorous
Consumes a dozen bolus
Memorize their dimensions
Understand their configuration
Remember their colour code
Yellow controls sugar
White maintains pressure
Pink prevents anemia
Red for anorexia
They keep your heart beating
Eyes from twitching
And throat from aching
Have them with breakfast lunch and dinner
Consider them as starters or dessert

12. Salute Our Soldiers

Soldiers are a country's wealth
Guard your nation and your wealth
Leave their homes to keep you safe
Stay in places you never dwell
Scale the terrain hard to trail
Eat the food you never accept
Valor is their middle name
Live for the nation and die for it
March forward and never retreat
Round the clock they are on guard
Keep you safe from enemies abroad
They are the pride of every heart
Salute them for their mettle and might
Bow to their parents for their sacrifice

13. Mama Dear

When your mama leaves you alone
To leave for an abode of her own
No crying and pleading will bring her back
She brought you to this world is an undeniable fact
Taught you the lesson which you now possess
Finished her duty and solemnly left
Follow the path she carved for you
Make her proud with the work you do
Life's lessons taught by her
Will haul you up when you are in a spot
Mama dear can never go
She is always there in your heart

14. Sunflower

In the morning I take a stroll
To wipe the slumber from my eyes
Stretch my legs and clear my bowels
See a golden flower in my stride
Waiting for the sun to rise
Blossoms with the heavenly light
Track the sun as it glides
"Sunflower" it's fondly called
Smitten with the golden rays
Bask itself with divine light
Love and devotion kept apart
Fills the floret one by one
With golden oil
Till the heads are done
The plant follows the mighty sun
To fill its bounty and raise its sons
Humbled by all this sight
To home I return with a vision
To start my day with a mission

15. The Storm

A storm is brewing in the east
Birds and animals seem to retreat
Air is still and nature has a solemn feel
Dark clouds conceal the pleasant land scape
Ghastly winds precede
Thunder and lightning give an eerie feel
Rain gushes down in torrents
The feeling you get is not so pleasant
Apprehension takes over common sense
And you sincerely wait for the drama to end

16. Evolution

Life on earth has never been the same
Micro to macro they went through change
Ant to man we travelled along
To evolve has been the natural way
Now we hear of camouflage
Transparent animals have come to stay
Invisibility is a trait they see,
Where glass wings have come to play
Butterflies, frogs and octopus have found their way
To elude the predators that come to prey
Its evolution on the way
What with man we cannot speculate.

17. Poetic Site

I have friends round the world
When it's morning its noon for some
Yet we meet daily once
To share our passion and our woes
As if we are just next door
Makes us feel the world is one
Hail the science that has this done
And "My poetic Side" for all the fun

18. Life's Journey Ahead

Life is a river that flows
Love is the boat on which you board
Select a boat which does not sink
Or capsize in a torrent of wind
Flow may be rough or smooth
Strength of the boat makes you dare
Take on board only people who care
Clean your boat to make it fair
Keep it safe from wear and tear
Paint afresh with time to spare
Let it sparkle in the light of love
Enjoy your life with every ripple
Twist and turns drive you mad
Calamities can make you sad
Friends and family keep you sane
So select your boat with love and care
Remember it's your life's journey ahead

19. Man Animal Conflict

Elephant on a rampage
Tiger on a prowl
Fox that eats the fowl
We call it man animal conflict
Why the animals behave so
To make our relations sore
Is it climate change or more?
Don't tempt them with your fowls
Leave a buffer zone, so they never prowl
Ensure their number never exceeds
So that both can live in peace.

20. Cob web

Cobwebs are beautiful structures
Made by little creatures
To trap the prey for their supper
Yet they represent an unused den
And now I ask you friends
Why do man get trapped in the "web" these days?
Go round and round with no escape
Lose sight of the beautiful landscape
Fail to communicate face to face
Will our lives shrink to a den?
Should children fall in this trend?
Maybe it's good for some and not for all
Moderation is all I ask for

21. In God's Court

The God I know is not always fair
Sometimes he treats as if I am not there
Maybe he knows things
Which I am not aware
I ask for justice for my toil and tear
He smiles at me with little care
Maybe his court is just as unfair
Or it's listed and just not there
Have to wait till judgment day
To appear before his honorable "Grace"
When I can plead the case my way
So patiently I wait
For a fair trial to settle my case

22. Spirituality

When I am in doubt
When my mind wonders about
When I am in pain
And look around in vain
For a pole
To lean with trust
For hope to push me forward
Then I see a light
Call it Ram, Allah or Jesus
A name for me to trust
A shoulder for me to weep
Clear my mind of fear and doubt
Fill my heart with love and hope
Helps me pass this woe
And thus I move about
With a little hope to start

23. Festivals

Festival days are random ones
Fill your life with laughter and fun
Friends and family gather around
Gifts and parcels make their round
Fasting and feasting are the major ones
Little traditions are called upon
To make the gathering a solemn one
Food you eat is not the normal one
Meet the people you miss in life
Laze around with little thought
And so we meet yearly once
To tell our children we are one

24. Adieu To The Sun

The Sun has moved away
To the southern hemisphere
To bless the life hither stay
Without his glare, winter is here to stay
As others should also have light
We wished him well on his trip away
With 'arthi' we bade him off
On 'Chat' the auspicious day
We'll welcome him back again
With prayers, sweets and fun
On "Sankranthi" as he turns around
And returns to give us warmth
This is how we were brought up
To respect nature in all its forms
Mountains, trees, rivers and air
Considered as blessings
Never to be exploited, but use with care
With due diligence and respect
We requested permission
From all life that stay in there
Before we use them for our daily ware
These gestures we forgot

Threw them out to be more civilized
Maybe it's time to restart
To appreciate the little blessings we have got
Not through gestures alone
But with rightful thoughts
Refrain from selfish ventures
Restrict our uses and never exploit
Prevent "Climate Change" which is patronized

**Chat and *Sankranthi are religious Indian festivals related to*
sun.

25. X- mas Grace

The sun or the moon
It's hard to say
From the east
He comes without a glare
So serene so calm
To show us he is up there
His might he has lost
To the winter flakes
That brings the X- mas Grace
Maybe it is for 'Santa'
The sun has taken this shape
As he comes from a very cold place
To bless us all and shower his grace
Enjoy the winter with gifts and cakes
And the blessings from the 'Holy Grace'

26. My Concept Of Love

Love is an abstract noun
It is seen all around
Does not confine to a single one
Manifests in different forms
Keeps you awake when your parents are down
Clasps the hand of your little one
Makes you flutter when your spouse is late
Puts a smile when your loved ones gain
Leaves you aghast when they are in pain
Manifests in different forms
Anger, duty, sacrifice or a routine you perform
Deny its existence you may
Beside whatever you say
Love keeps the world moving around
Friendship, devotion, respect are different forms

27. Hail The Crow

Crows are sacred birds
Represent departed souls
Dressed in black you see her around
Flies about with a beseeching sound
Make you feel that someone is around
Alarm clocks need not run
Wake you up when the sun is out
Eat the food you throw away
Cleans your courtyard from rats and mice
Claims her authority over pigeons and fowls
Keeps an eye on things around
Gives a warning when something prowls.
I saw her on a banana bunch
To devour the insects seen around
She is a friend and not a foe
So we feed her yearly once
As gratitude to our departed ones.

In Hindu mythology crows are considered as representatives of our departed souls It's customary to feed the crows on remembrance day.

28. Bridal Bouquet

Bridal Bouquet in my garden

Needs a string to keep it right

Or a tree to make it straight

I wonder why it's called a bridal bouquet

For its beauty or its plight

Does a lady need a guy?

To keep her straight or support her by

A learned girl can lead a life

Without a family to make it tight

Worldly riches can leave you starved

Love and support lighten your path

Have a partner who is right

To share your sorrows when things are tight

Enjoy your happiness when life is bright

*Let the *bridal bouquet bloom away*

I'll give it support to make it stay

**A climber with beautiful flowers*

29. Wild Boar

Wild boar enters the field
Tampers with the crop
Leaves the farmer aghast
To see his labour lost
Time and money spend
Is not the boar's concern
They come in troops
Trample the field in just a run
It's not for food, just for fun
Time to declare war
Keep the boar at bay
Or things will be out of hand
And people will have to leave the land
Take this up in Parliament
Save the farmer if you can
Farming and conservation should go hand in hand

30. Gain Vs Losses

We work to gain all our lives

What we lose, we never highlight

Acquired skills make you bright

Helps you scale the heights with might

Learn to walk, nobody bothers to carry you about

Learn to drive and you no longer walk

And miss the friends that were part of your walk

Get a job and lose your freedom

Build a house and be rooted to a spot

Count your gains and your losses pile up

You reach a stage when nothing matters much

Gains no longer hold their charm

But losses you shall recount

Gains you worked for all your life

Losses you cherish more in the sunset of your life

31. Love Thy Neighbours

Neighbours are your closest friends
Share the air and the land
To become enemies is the normal trend
Where we went wrong we don't understand
Selfishness, jealousy or intolerance
All these and others might lend a hand
To cause a dent which is hard to mend
Wage a war for the smallest spark
And feel the brunt for this stunt
Others far away may fuel the fight
To see the neighbours fall apart
And lick the gains from the fallout
Loss of life and property is not their concern
Never be a ladle in their hands
"Do unto others what you would like others to do unto you"
Follow this mantra to make your neighbor your bosom friend.

32. Land Of The Lost

As I loiter in the land of the lost
Come across a lot many souls
Family, friends, lovers and acquaintance
All of them are there to hold
As they pop up from the lost little hole
I scan them through the network mode
And there they are in my face book post
To say hello, from long ago
Which makes retirement a glorious one
With time and leisure we can go for a witch-hunt
Pick up the strings we lost on the way
And make our lives colorful again

33. Land Of Poorams

In God's own country
It's a common sight
To see the elephants
Decked up bright
With golden head gear
And satin umbrellas
Adorn the Gods
When they take a ride
To bless the people
From their mighty heights
Trumpets and drums
Follow their strides
In a procession
They make their rounds
Streets and houses brighten up
Children and adults line up
To welcome the procession
As they pass
Our summer days have their charms
With colorful 'Poorams' all around

"Poorams" are temple rituals celebrated during summer months. Thrissur pooram is the largest temple festival in Kerala.

34. The Squirrel And The Bird

Squirrel and bird had a fight
To eat a fruit that was just ripe
Squirrel ran up the tree to make his claim
Bird zoomed down to put up a fight
The sound they made was a noisy squabble
Their little fight was a visual delight
Squirrel hopped about and rebuked the bird
As a fluffy tail went up and down
Chirping bird fluttered around with yellow wings
Ready to peck the squirrel in its stride
The nasty brawl lasted some time
The squirrel had his way and ate his share
Hopped away to end the fight
Bird picked at the fruit and flew away
Farmer stood aside to see the duo fight
His toil is to feed the world- man or animal it's just alike

35. Save The Planet

Nature holds secrets unknown
To decipher it is a challenge of its own
Who would think the sand from 'Sahara'
Will find its way to the 'Amazon'
Heat at the 'Equator'
Would make the 'Trade winds' blow
Water currents of the 'Pacific'
Will heat and cool the earth you know
A depression here and a depression there
Will make the rains move everywhere
Tend our 'Planet' with love and care
'Chaos Theory' says
"Little changes here and there
Can cause the people lot of woes"
The 'Butterfly effect' is there to hold
May our deeds be sacred so
To save the 'Planet' and keep it whole
For our children when we go

36. Train journey

Peering through the window pane
Awake in the dark on a moving train
Beautiful cities passing by
Thrill the heart of a lonely soul
A starless night, a lustrous sight
Of moving cars with glaring lights
Lines of light that brighten streets
Colorful neon's that score the heights
Dazzling sight like a shooting star
Gladden the heart of a lonely soul
Awake on a train that moves so fast

37. Fantasy

If I were a seagull I will stretch my wings and fly
Far into the sea to enjoin the silence of the ocean
If I were a crane I will launch into the blue sky
Flap my wings and fly to places far away
If I were a butterfly I will flutter around the bushes
Sing a song to the flowers as I fly
If I were a hawk I will soar over the mountains
Enjoy the greenery of the earth and the life moving by
If I were a vulture I'll fly above the sand dunes
And look for the oasis of life
If I were a whale, I'll plunge into ocean
To see the beauty of life
But I am a human with no wings or fins to fly and dive
Yet my deeds are crooked enough
To mar the beauty and the life

38. My Little Brother

Being a sister is not so easy
With a brother who is an 'Elf' to start
With love and patience I do retort
Sense and reason is not for his sort
Rashness and violence is all he knows
Shielding him from harm is arduous to all
A game with him will end in war
Screams at me and pulls my hair
Tears my books and breaks my dolls
Scolding I get is not always fair
At last I retreat with a broken heart
The angelic smile on his sleeping face
Wipes the remorse for all his deeds
Clinches the love from my little heart

39. My Elder Sis

Elder Sister is a bore
Treats me as a serf, dictates as a Chief
Tests my patience with all these deeds
My cars and guns she does not care
Shopping and cooking are hard to brace
A game with her makes me flare
I lose my control and scratch her hair
Babies and dolls need love and care
Chatter and tantrums are hard to bear
A little cockroach makes her scared
Leave her alone is all I hear
Sheds her tears when I am caned
Holds my hands when I am in pain
I feel secure with her around
Love my sister with all her faults
She'll be there when I am in a spot

40. The Nest

Just above the window sill
There was a nest with two little bills
Fluttering parents fussed about
With little grubs in their beak
To snuff the chirping of the fowls
And quench the clamor for the grubs
Up and down they made their rounds
In and out I saw them dart
Noisy household made me scold
To hear the chirping day and night
Raising kids is a tedious task
Bird or man it's just alike
One day the chirping stopped
The lovely birds had flown apart
Leaving the nest that had played its part
Today as my children depart
I feel appalled to see them off
Then the little nest on the loft
Reminds me its nature's path

41. Kite

I had a kite which soared the heights
To see vistas far away
The pride I felt is nothing to say
To see it fly up in the sky
The splendid kite looked so bright
As it soared to greater heights
A gust of wind snapped the string
Control of the kite was whisked away
Heavy wind blew it apart
To places far away
Wonder why I lost my kite
Was it the height or the wind?
Or maybe the strength of the string.
At times things are just the way
Moderation makes them stay
As they go high they fly away
And we tend to lose them from site

42. Teachers Day

Teachers' day is celebrated with splendor
For the toil they put and their zealous venture
Every teacher is a model to say
Some teach you how to care
Others teach you what to spare
With gratitude we remember
The way they ridiculed our slumber
Punishments meted out for our blunders
Science and maths that made us wonder
The doors they opened for us to ponder
The old and the new that took us yonder
Hand in hand they took us up the ranks
To start our lives with grandeur

43. Cars Or Stars

The sky is full of stars
I rarely see them now
As the air is full of dust
Which blurs the vision up
Diamonds in the sky
Seem a vision of the past
To buy the cars we ride
The jewels we had to part
The junk we fill around
Will deplete us of the gold
Cars have made our lives
Much easier than the old
Trading is what we do
To live a life of ease
Regrets we should not hold
Its trade off for our goals.

44. The Lotus

Lotus is a flower that forms
The seat of many sacred souls
Why Gods find it so
Makes us ponder about its role
In a pool of dirt it grows
Its origin is far too old
Arising from dirt it may
Purity is never at stake
Grandeur it maintains
No dirt sticks to the plant
Drops of water roll away
From the leaf
As if to say
Where you are born is just your fate
What you do makes you great.

45. Dilemma

Sometimes it's difficult to put things right
However much you think otherwise
At times it is the life of a person so dear
There is a limit to which you can interfere
When people are close you feel the brunt
Helplessness that makes you numb
Lend a shoulder for them to rest
Hold their hands when they need rest
Leave the rest for them to solve
And choose the path which they feel best

46. Mistletoes

Mistletoes bless the X- mas days
Bonds they form are strong to say
Wind and gale will never break them away
Represent life on leafless branches
With not a leaf or flower to sway
Even on bleak winter days
Stay attached all the way
Feed the birds and save the day
Show us how people should stay
Bonded in misery and sunshine days

47. Tantrums

Tantrums —a common course of action
Where children are in motion
A little trigger is all you need
To start a spiteful reaction
Time- uncertain
Mornings and bed times vulnerable occasions
Like a volcano it erupts at intermission
Tests the mother's patience
When words and deeds fail to quench the passion
And "ignore" has no action
A meltdown may be the reaction
The household becomes a scene of action
Father flies in with his round of action
To quench the raging storm,
With threats, might and a diplomatic mission
You remember all these stressful days
When your grandchildren come to stay
And smile at this daily chore
Which formed the routine
In your youthful days.

48. Love Or Might

Warriors, kings and dynasties
Ruled the earth for years
None of them could make a dent
In the minds of the people they tend
Thrones, castles, forts and palaces
Are the only relics that meant
Such people ruled our den.
People who tended cows and sheep
Through Love and wisdom
Conquered the hearts of men
They built no castles or forts
Yet across the world
Temples, churches and mosques are built
To remember their lives and teachings
And sing the praises of these men.

49. Gowardhan Giridhari

Gowardhana giridhari
Is Krishna by the way
Because he told his father
Pray not Indra the rain God
Pray the mountains
And your rains will stay
The mountains enrich the clouds
That brings the rain your way
Angry rain God made him pay
With thunder and lightning
And rains that lashed for days
Plunge man and beast to slay
With his finger
Krishna lifted the mountain
Kept his clan and cattle
Safe from the fury of nature
His teachings to the people
Was simple and straight
Protect your nature
And your climate will not stray.

50. A Matter Of The Heart

Sometimes it is hard to refrain
From the throngs of pain
That engulfs you in vain
And causes a lot of strain

51. How Grandma Spoilt Her Son

Little Grandma had a son
Her boy was pampered much
Which made the people stunt
To see a boy so dump
Kept him in a rundown farm
Fed him lots of bun
To drink he had lots of rum
Which made him a lazy little lump
One day Grandma left the world
Leaving her son alone
The lazy little son
Found no work or fun
He left the barn
. To fend the cows and goats
But knew not how to fend
The farm and its hen
His mother was to blame
For she taught him not a thing
Too much love made him sink
To the rotten state He was in

52. On The Move

Travelling around the world is no longer a myth
Perth, Peru and Port Blair are all within reach
Buy your tickets, board the plane
Fasten your seat belts and there you go
Sailing through the skies
With the cottony clouds moving around
Over the bright blue sea, rivers, trees and houses
And the mountains below
Make the vision a picturesque sight.
Varied lands, varied cultures, varied food, fun and dance
Will make your travel a cherished one
Hurry, hurry do not delay
The hyper loop is on its way
To make you travel faster by day
From end to end they move so fast
And lose sight of your travel path
So off you go without delay

53. Road To Heaven

I am in search of a road
A road that leads to heaven
There are many to direct the way
But all the roads are strewn
With roadblocks to test your mission
Which questions your vision
And you back out with frustration
Then I listen to my heart
Heaven is but a Utopia
Why not make one here
So I currently live in heaven
With sunshine and rains to lighten my days
Trees and plants to freshen the air
Birds and flowers to brighten the place
Friends and neighbours
Who care and share
Why go in search of heaven
Make one in your garden

54. Rainbow

Rainbow stretches across the sky
Violet, indigo, blue, green yellow, orange, red
They make a pretty sight
Colorful rainbow is a spectral light
Where all the colors seem so bright
As they blend they seem as white
And fill the world with heat and light
Would we like to see them run,
As different colors or a single one
Colors alone enchant our hearts
When they merge they serve us right
What we learn from all this sight
To act as one for all the might.

55. My Better Half

It's hard to say we think the same
To the contrary, we may claim
As you are from Mars and I am from Venus
Beyond our thoughts, there is a plane
Where both of us are one and the same
The mystic bond that binds within
Is hard to break even if we think
With malice to none, we crossed our swords
A daily ritual it was thought
Now in the twilight of our lives
With nothing much to go about
We find no reason to spark a fight
And our children have made their flight

I thank my readers for their patience and support. Hope you enjoyed my musings.

www.ingramcontent.com/pod-product-compliance
Lightning Source LLC
Chambersburg PA
CBHW021132130726
47988CB00003B/1263